EXPLORE THE
FANTASTIC WORLD OF

INSECTS AND BUGS

PICTURE ENCYCLOPEDIA

Wonder House

DUNG BEETLE

The Dung Beetle is a small, hardworking insect with a shiny, metallic body that can be black, brown or even green. There are different types of Dung Beetles, including rollers, tunnelers and dwellers. These beetles feed mainly on animal dung, which they roll into balls and bury to eat or lay their eggs inside. Dung Beetles range in size from 0.1–2.5in (0.2–6.3cm). They can weigh up to 3.5oz (99g). A Dung Beetle can live up to 2 years. Belonging to the family ***Scarabaeidae***, these helpful bugs play a big role in cleaning up nature by recycling animal waste!

DID YOU KNOW?

Dung Beetles can roll balls of poop that are 50 times their weight!

LADYBUG

The Ladybug, often called a Ladybird Beetle, is a small, colorful insect. They are usually bright red or orange with black spots, although some can be yellow or even black. Ladybugs belong to the beetle family, specifically the Coccinellidae family. These friendly bugs love to eat aphids. They are about 0.3–0.4in (0.7–1cm) long. A Ladybug can live for 2–3 years. Their scientific name is ***Coccinella septempunctata***, which means "seven-spotted Ladybug."

DID YOU KNOW?

A Ladybug can eat up to 5,000 aphids in its lifetime!

STAG BEETLE

The Stag Beetle is a fascinating insect known for its impressive mandibles that resemble the antlers of a stag. These beetles are typically black or brown, and males often have larger jaws than females. They are herbivores, feeding mainly on tree sap and decaying wood. Stag Beetles can grow up to 1.3–3in (3.3–7.6cm) long, with males being larger than females. Once they become an adult, they live for around 4 months. They belong to the family ***Lucanidae***, and their scientific name is ***Lucanus cervus***.

DID YOU KNOW?

Their larvae, baby Stag Beetles, live underground for a long time before becoming adults.

WEEVIL

Weevils are small beetles known for their long snouts. They come in various colors like brown, black and gray, with some having red or yellow markings. There are many types of Weevils, but the most common are grain and rice Weevils. They eat plants, grains and seeds, often damaging crops. Weevils are tiny, measuring about 0.1–3in (0.2–7.6cm) long, and weigh even less than an ounce. Their average lifespan is about 3–4 months; their survival period depends upon the temperature. Weevils belong to the beetle family ***Curculionidae***.

DID YOU KNOW?

They can destroy food items like nuts and grains by drilling a hole and laying their eggs inside them.

GROUND BEETLE

The Ground Beetle is usually black or dark brown, though some species can be metallic or brightly colored. These beetles are found all over the world. Ground Beetles are carnivorous, feeding mostly on other insects like caterpillars, ants and spiders. They are small, typically measuring around 1.5in (3.8cm) but some species may exceed the size. Ground Beetles can live for approximately 2–3 years. They are known for their quick movements and strong jaws, making them excellent hunters. The scientific name for this family of beetles is ***Carabidae***.

DID YOU KNOW?

Some Ground Beetles produce a foul-smelling liquid to disgust away predators!

RHINOCEROS BEETLE

The Rhinoceros Beetle is a large, powerful insect known for the horn on its head, which looks like a rhino's horn! They are usually dark brown or black in color. Rhinoceros Beetles eat rotting wood, fruit and tree sap. They can grow up to 6in (15.2cm) long, though they are strong for their size. Rhinoceros Beetles live around 1–2 years. They belong to the ***Scarabaeidae*** family and subfamily ***Dynastinae***. These beetles are harmless and are also kept as pets.

DID YOU KNOW?

The males use their horns to compete for females for mating.

LONG-HORNED BEETLE

The Long-Horned Beetle is a colorful insect with long antennae, often longer than its body. They come in many colors, including black, brown, yellow and red. There are over 35,000 species of Long-Horned Beetles! They are mostly herbivores, feeding on wood, leaves and plant stems. Long-Horned Beetles can grow up to 6in (15.2cm) long, though most are smaller. Their lifespan is about 1–2 years, depending on the species. These beetles belong to the family ***Cerambycidae***, comprising thousands of species.

DID YOU KNOW?

Their larvae eat wood, thus helping to break down dead trees.

JEWEL BEETLE

The Jewel Beetle is a shiny, colorful insect with wings of vibrant hues like metallic green, blue and purple. Jewel Beetles feed on plants, especially leaves, flowers and wood. They are about 0.1–3in (0.2–7.6cm) in long and weigh very little, usually less than an ounce. Their lifespan varies but is typically around 1–3 years. These beetles belong to the family ***Buprestidae*** and are known for their hard, glossy shell. These beetles are admired for their beautiful appearance and are often found in tropical regions.

DID YOU KNOW?

The bright blue-green wings of Jewel Beetles help them camouflage and hide from predators.

TIGER BEETLE

The Tiger Beetle is a brightly colored insect known for its metallic blue, green or orange body with stripes or spots. Tiger Beetles are fast runners and wait near their burrows to chase down their prey, which consists of small insects like ants and spiders. They range in size from 0.5–1in (1.2–2.5cm) long. Tiger Beetles live for about 1–3 years. These beetles are fierce hunters, using their sharp mandibles to catch food. Their scientific name is ***Cicindelidae***. They love sunny, sandy areas where they can move freely.

DID YOU KNOW?

Tiger Beetles can run up to 5.5mph (8.9kph), making them one of the fastest insects!

BLACK BUG

The Black Bug, also known as the Black Aphid, is usually small and dark, with a shiny black color. These bugs are herbivores, feeding on plant sap, especially from beans and other crops. They are tiny, about 0.08–0.1in (0.2–0.3cm) long, and weigh very little, even less than an ounce. Their lifespan is short, lasting only a few weeks, but they can reproduce quickly and live in large groups. They belong to the ***Aphididae*** family, and their scientific name is ***Aphis fabae***.

DID YOU KNOW?

Black Bugs come in all shapes and sizes, from tiny ants to big beetles!

SPITTLEBUG

The Spittlebug is a small, green or brown insect. These insects are herbivores, feeding on plant sap. Spittlebugs are about 0.2–0.5in (0.5–1.2cm) long. They are known for the white, frothy foam they produce, which protects their nymphs as they develop. Their lifespan is usually around a year, with most of their life spent as nymphs hidden in the foam. They belong to the family ***Cercopidae*** and their scientific name is ***Cercopis vulnerata***.

DID YOU KNOW?

Spittlebugs are also called froghoppers for their high jumps.

RED STINK BUG

The Red Stink Bug is a colorful insect that features a striking red body with black markings. Red Stink Bugs are herbivores, feeding on plant juices, especially from fruits and vegetables. They can grow to be about 0.5in (1.2cm) long and typically weigh around 0.02oz (556mg). These bugs have a lifespan of about 6–12 months. When threatened, they release a strong odor to protect themselves, which is why they are called stink bugs! They are scientifically known as ***Cosmopepla lintneriana*** and belong to the family ***Pentatomidae***, which is known for its shield-shaped bugs.

DID YOU KNOW?

Red Stink Bugs undergo incomplete metamorphosis, meaning they look the same even as they grow.

SEED BUG

The Seed Bug is a small insect that usually has a color range of brown to black, often with striking patterns. Seed Bugs are herbivores, feeding primarily on seeds, as is evident by their name. They are typically about 0.2–0.4in (0.5–1cm) long. Their lifespan can be up to a year. Seed Bugs can often be found in gardens or fields, playing an important role in the ecosystem by helping to disperse seeds. They belong to the family ***Lygaeidae***. Their scientific name is ***Lygaeus kalmii***.

DID YOU KNOW?

The letter X forms on their back when they fold their wings.

BUFFALO TREEHOPPER

The Buffalo Treehopper is a fascinating bug known for its striking green or brown color and unique shape, resembling a small buffalo. This hemipteran insect feeds on plant sap, making it a herbivore. It typically measures about 0.3in (0.8cm) long. A Buffalo Treehopper can often be seen hopping around gardens and fields. As a member of the ***Membracidae*** family, its scientific name is ***Stictocephala bubalus***.

DID YOU KNOW?

They can injure orchard trees, especially apple trees.

SQUASH BUG

The Squash Bug is a dark brown or black insect with orange or yellow markings. Squash Bugs are about 0.5–0.7in (1.2–1.9cm) long. They feed on the sap of plants, especially squash and pumpkins, often harming gardens. Their lifespan is around 3–4 months. They are a type of true bug belonging to the family ***Coreidae***, and their scientific name is ***Anasa tristis***.

DID YOU KNOW?

Female Squash Bugs can lay up to 200 eggs at once, usually on the underside of leaves.

NORTHERN GIANT HORNET

The Northern Giant Hornet is a fascinating insect. They have a striking color with a dark brown body and bright yellow-orange markings on their faces and legs. These hornets are social insects that live in colonies and primarily feed on other insects, particularly honeybees. They can grow to be about 2in (5cm) long, making them one of the largest hornets in the world, and weigh around 0.1oz (2.9g). They have a lifespan of about a year. Belonging to the family ***Vespidae***, the Northern Giant Hornet plays an essential role in its ecosystem. They are scientifically known as ***Vespa mandarinia***.

HUNCHBACK BEE FLY

The Hunchback Bee Fly is a fascinating insect that looks like a bumblebee! They have a fuzzy, yellow-and-black body and is about 1in (2.5cm) long. These flies love to feed on nectar from flowers, using their long proboscis to sip the sweet liquid. They have a short lifespan, usually living for only a few weeks. These amazing flies are known for their unique hunchbacked appearance, which helps them stand out among other insects. The Hunchback Bee Fly belongs to the ***Bombyliidae*** family and their scientific name is ***Anthrax anthrax***.

DID YOU KNOW?

Hunchback Bee Flies are great pollinators and help flowers grow by spreading pollen.

CELLOPHANE BEE

The Cellophane Bee is a small, colorful insect. They have a fuzzy, black-and-yellow body with shiny, translucent wings. These bees are also called plasterer bees. They get their name from the way they line their nests with a waterproof, cellophane-like substance. Cellophane Bees feed on nectar and pollen from flowers. They are about 0.5in (1.2cm) long and weigh less than 0.04oz (1g). Their lifespan is usually a few weeks in the wild. They belong to the ***Colletidae*** family of the genus ***Colletes***.

HONEYBEE

The Honeybee is a small, buzzing insect with black and yellow stripes that help it blend in with flowers. There are different types of Honeybees, but the most common is the Western Honeybee. Honeybees eat nectar and pollen from flowers, which also helps plants grow by spreading pollen. They are famous for making sweet honey. They are about 0.5in (1.2cm) long and weigh less than an ounce! Worker Honeybees live for a few weeks, while the queen can live for about 5 years. They belong to the ***Apidae*** family. The scientific name for the Honeybee is ***Apis mellifera***.

DID YOU KNOW?

Honeybees can flap their wings about 200 times per second!

ARAFED BEE

The Arafed Bee is a small, black- and yellow-striped bee known for its hardworking nature. They feed on nectar and pollen from flowers, helping plants grow through pollination. Arafed Bees are about 0.5in (1.2cm) long and weigh less than 0.01oz (0.3g). They can live for around 6 weeks. These bees belong to the family ***Apidae*** and have the scientific name ***Apis arafedensis***.

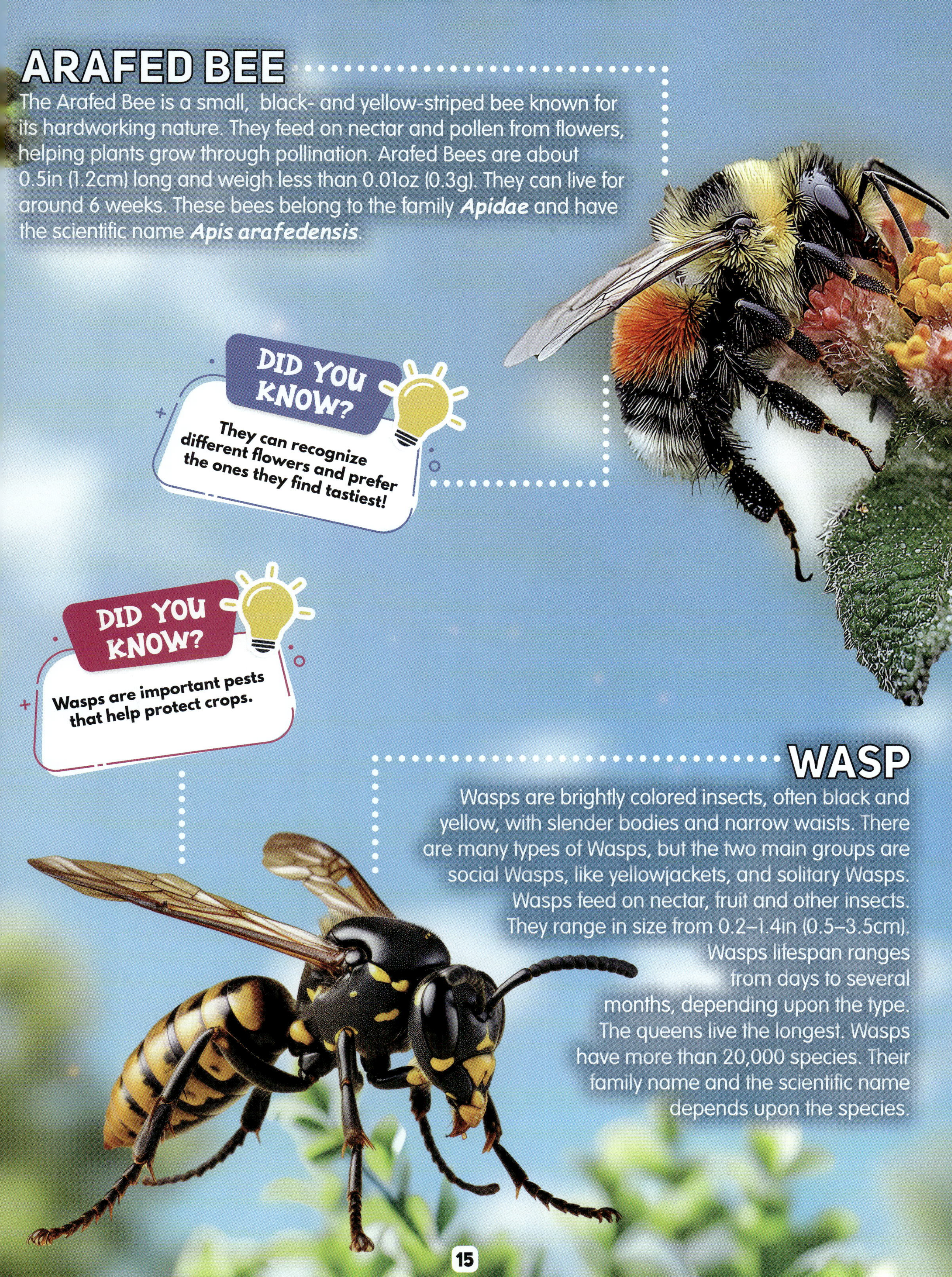

DID YOU KNOW?

They can recognize different flowers and prefer the ones they find tastiest!

DID YOU KNOW?

Wasps are important pests that help protect crops.

WASP

Wasps are brightly colored insects, often black and yellow, with slender bodies and narrow waists. There are many types of Wasps, but the two main groups are social Wasps, like yellowjackets, and solitary Wasps. Wasps feed on nectar, fruit and other insects. They range in size from 0.2–1.4in (0.5–3.5cm). Wasps lifespan ranges from days to several months, depending upon the type. The queens live the longest. Wasps have more than 20,000 species. Their family name and the scientific name depends upon the species.

FRUIT FLY

The Fruit Fly is a tiny insect known for its reddish-brown or yellow color with bright red eyes. Fruit flies are about 0.125in (3.1mm) long and weigh almost nothing! They feed on ripe or decaying fruits, making them a common sight in kitchens. They only live about 40–50 days but reproduce quickly. They belong to the ***Drosophilidae*** and ***Trypetidae*** families. Their scientific name varies according to the species.

DID YOU KNOW?

Fruit Flies are used by scientists to study genetics and inheritance.

HOUSEFLY

The Housefly is a small insect with a grayish-black body and large red eyes. They eat decaying food, garbage and even animal waste. They are about 0.25in (6.3mm) long. Their lifespan is usually around 15–25 days. Houseflies are very common and can be found all around the world. They are a member of the ***Muscidae*** family and their scientific name is ***Musca domestica***.

DID YOU KNOW?

Houseflies have a superb sense of smell and can detect food from over a mile away!

MOSQUITO

The Mosquito is a small flying insect known for its black, grayish-brown color with long, slender legs. As a bloodsucking pest, its diet mainly consists of nectar from flowers and the blood of animals, including humans. Mosquitoes typically measure around 0.1–0.6in (3–16mm) in size and weigh about 0.04gr (2.5mg). Their average lifespan varies from 2 weeks to a few months. Mosquitoes belong to the ***Culicidae*** family, and comprises thousands of species each having a different scientific name.

DID YOU KNOW?

Mosquitoes have been around for over 100 million years, even when dinosaurs existed.

GREAT GREEN BUSH-CRICKET

The Great Green Bush-Cricket is a vibrant insect with a bright green body, perfect for blending among leaves and bushes. This insect is a herbivore, feeding on leaves, flowers and sometimes small insects. The Great Green Bush-Cricket is about 2–3in (5–7.6cm) long. It can live for about 6 months, starting as eggs in the winter. With its long antennae and strong hind legs, it is a great jumper and loves to hide in tall grass or shrubs! It belongs to the ***Tettigoniidae*** family, and its scientific name is ***Tettigonia viridissima***.

DID YOU KNOW?

The nymphs or tiny Green Bush-Crickets do not have wings.

FIELD CRICKET

The Field Cricket is a small insect with a shiny black or dark brown body. Field Crickets are omnivores, eating plants, seeds and small insects. They grow up to 1in (2.5cm) long and barely weigh anything. Their lifespan is short, usually lasting around 3 months. These crickets are known for their loud chirping, which they use to communicate, especially during warm summer evenings. They are often found in fields, gardens and grassy areas. They belong to the family ***Gryllidae***, and are members of the genus ***Gryllus***.

DID YOU KNOW?

Field Crickets are also commonly called black crickets.

MOLE CRICKET

The Mole Cricket is a brown insect with a velvety body and strong, spade-like front legs that are perfect for digging. These insects are omnivores, eating roots, plants and small insects. They are about 1–2in (2.5-5cm) long and weigh less than 0.1oz (2.8g) Mole Crickets live for about 1–2 years. They spend most of their time underground, using their legs to burrow through soil. They belong to the family ***Gryllotalpidae***, and their scientific name depends upon the species.

DID YOU KNOW?

Mole Crickets can dig soil around 8in (20cm) deep.

AMERICAN BIRD GRASSHOPPER

The American Bird Grasshopper is a large grasshopper with a body that can be green, brown or gray, with spotted wings and black markings. These grasshoppers are herbivores, meaning they feed on plants like grass, leaves and crops. They can grow up to 2.5–3in (6.3–7.6cm) long. The American Bird Grasshoppers have a lifespan of about 6 months. These insects are great jumpers and can also fly; often found in fields, gardens and open spaces in warm regions. They belong to the family ***Acrididae*** and their scientific name is ***Schistocerca americana***.

DID YOU KNOW?

American Bird Grasshoppers can jump up to 20 times their body length!

MEADOW GRASSHOPPER

The Meadow Grasshopper is a bright-green insect with a brown or reddish back and long legs for jumping. These grasshoppers are herbivores, feeding on grasses and plants. They are about 0.6–0.9in (1.5–2.3cm) long. Their lifespan is typically a year. Meadow Grasshoppers are common in fields and meadows, where they hop around, blending into the grass to stay safe from predators. They belong to the family ***Acrididae***, and their scientific name is ***Chorthippus parallelus***.

DID YOU KNOW?

They love to sing by rubbing their back legs against their wings.

SPUR-THROATED GRASSHOPPER

The Spur-Throated Grasshopper is usually brown or green, helping it blend into its grassy surroundings. These grasshoppers are herbivores, meaning they eat plants, especially leaves and grasses. They grow to about 1.5–2in (3.8–5cm) long. Their lifespan is typically around a few months. They get their name from the spine-like bump between their front legs. They belong to the ***Acrididae*** family and the subfamily ***Cyrtacanthacridinae***, and their scientific name depends upon the species.

DID YOU KNOW?

Spur-Throated Grasshoppers are commonly found in North America.

GIANT KATYDID

The Giant Katydid is one of the largest katydids and is usually green, helping it look just like a leaf. Herbivores by nature, Giant Katydids feed on leaves, flowers and fruit. They can grow up to 6in (15.2cm) long, making them one of the largest katydid species. Despite their size, they only weigh around 0.8–1.2oz (22.6–34g). Their lifespan lasts about a few months to a year. Giant katydids are known for their incredible camouflage, hiding from predators in the trees! These amazing insects belong to the ***Tettigoniidae*** family, and their scientific name is ***Stilpnochlora couloniana***.

DID YOU KNOW?

They can "talk" to each other using sound waves!

CONE-HEADED KATYDID

The Cone-Headed Katydid is a fascinating insect with bright green or brown coloring, allowing it to blend in with the leaves. This herbivore primarily eats grass and leaves. It grows to about 1.5–2in (3.8–5cm) long. Weighing around 0.05oz (1.4g). A Cone-Headed Katydid is known for its distinctive cone-shaped head. Its lifespan typically lasts about 2–3 months, and it is often heard chirping at night. It belongs to the ***Tettigoniidae*** family and is scientifically known as ***Neoconocephalus retusus***.

DID YOU KNOW?

Cone-Headed Katydids can fly, but they prefer to hop around more than flying.

COMMON TRUE KATYDID

The Common True Katydid is bright green, helping it blend in with the leaves. Their wings resemble leaves. These insects are herbivores, meaning they eat plant leaves. They grow to about 2–2.5in (5–6.3cm) in size and weighs around 0.02–0.03oz (0.5–0.8g). They belong to the ***Tettigoniidae*** family, and their scientific name is ***Pterophylla camellifolia***.

DID YOU KNOW?

Their song sounds like they are saying "katy did, katy didn't...", which is how they got their name!

BLUE DASHER

The Blue Dasher is a striking dragonfly known for its bright blue body and greenish eyes. Generally, the males are blue and females have black and yellow stripes. These fascinating insects are often found near ponds and streams. Blue Dashers primarily eat smaller insects, using their sharp eyesight to catch prey mid-flight. They typically grow to about 2–2.5in (5–6.3cm) long. With a lifespan of about a year, these agile flyers are known for their vibrant colors and impressive flying skills. They belong to the family ***Libellulidae*** and their scientific name is ***Pachydiplax longipennis***.

DID YOU KNOW?

They start their life as aquatic nymphs underwater.

DID YOU KNOW?

Ebony Jewelwings can fold their wings while resting!

EBONY JEWELWING

The Ebony Jewelwing is a beautiful damselfly known for its shiny black wings and metallic green-blue body. These damselflies are carnivores, feeding on small insects like mosquitoes and gnats. They are around 1.5–2in (3.8–5cm) long, with delicate, slender bodies. They have a short lifespan, living only a few weeks to a few months. These graceful damselflies are often found near streams and ponds, fluttering slowly as they hunt for food. They belong to the family ***Calopterygidae***, and their scientific name is ***Calopteryx maculata***.

COMMON DARTER

The Common Darter is a small dragonfly with bright red or orange color males and yellowish-brown females. They are carnivores, eating small insects like mosquitoes, flies and other bugs. Common Darters measure about 1.3–1.5in (3.3–3.8cm) in length, with a wingspan of up to 2in (5cm). These dragonflies have a short lifespan of around 7–8 weeks. They are excellent hunters and can be found near ponds, lakes and slow rivers. These dragonflies belong to the family ***Libellulidae***, and their scientific name is ***Sympetrum striolatum***.

DID YOU KNOW?

Common Darters are expert at flying and can even fly backward!

PRAYING MANTIS

The Praying Mantis is a fascinating insect, usually green or brown in color, which helps it blend with plants. These insects are carnivores, meaning they eat other insects like flies, grasshoppers and even small lizards or birds! Praying Mantises are about 2–5in (5–12.7cm) long. They have a short lifespan, living about a year. Known for their long, bent front legs that look like they are praying. They can also use their legs to "bridge" gaps between leaves or branches, showing off their incredible hunting skills. They belong to the ***Mantidae*** family, and their scientific name depends upon the species

DID YOU KNOW?

A Praying Mantis can turn its head almost 180 degrees to look around!

DEVIL'S FLOWER MANTIS

The Devil's Flower Mantis is a striking insect that mimics a flower. It's a carnivore, feeding on small insects. The Devil's Flower Mantis can grow up to 5in (12.7cm) long and is quite lightweight, around 0.02oz (0.5g). Its lifespan is about 12 months. It's known for its camouflage skills—spreading its limbs and body to mimic a flower, and lure prey within its reach. This mantis belongs to the ***Empusidae*** family, and its scientific name is ***Idolomantis diabolica***.

DID YOU KNOW?

The Female Devil's Flower Mantises are much larger in size than the males.

ORCHID FLOWER MANTIS

The Orchid Mantis is a beautiful insect that looks like a flower, with colors like white, pink and purple. This mantis is a carnivore, eating insects like flies and bees. It can grow up to 2–3in (5–7.6cm) long and weighs about 0.01oz (0.3g). It lives for around 6–12 months. It is known for "bridging" gaps between leaves by using its long legs to reach its next hiding spot! It belongs to the ***Mantidae*** family, and its scientific name is ***Hymenopus coronatus***.

DID YOU KNOW?

They have excellent vision and can see in 3D, which helps them catch their food.

SPINY LEAF INSECT

The Spiny Leaf Insect is a unique insect with a rough, spiky body that is usually brown or green, helping it look like a twig or branch. These insects are herbivores, feeding mainly on leaves from plants like eucalyptus. They can grow up to 8in (20.3cm) long. Spiny Leaf Insects have a lifespan of about 12–18 months. Their spiny appearance helps them blend with trees, keeping them safe from predators. They belong to the ***Phasmatidae*** family, and their scientific name is ***Extatosoma tiaratum***.

DID YOU KNOW?

They wave their arms to drive away their predators.

LEAF INSECT

The Leaf Insect resembles a real leaf! Their color ranges from bright green to brown, helping them hide from predators in the forest. Leaf Insects are herbivores, which means they eat leaves, especially from trees and shrubs. They can grow up to 4in (10cm) long. Their average lifespan is about 6–12 months. These insects are experts at blending in with their leafy surroundings, making them masters of disguise. They belong to the ***Phylliidae*** family, and their scientific name depends on the species.

DID YOU KNOW?

Males of this family tend to be smaller in size than the females.

GIANT WALKINGSTICK

The Giant Walkingstick is a long, thin insect that is usually brown or green, helping it look just like a twig! These insects are herbivores, meaning they eat leaves and other plant parts. They can grow as long as 7in (17.8cm), making them one of the largest stick insects in North America. They can live for up to 2 years. When they move, they look like a twig swaying in the wind. They belong to the ***Diapheromeridae*** family, and their scientific name is ***Megaphasma denticrus***.

DID YOU KNOW?

Unlike some insects, they don't sting or bite; they rely on their camouflage for protection.

MONARCH BUTTERFLY

The Monarch Butterfly is famous for its bright orange and black wings with white spots. Monarchs are herbivores, feeding on nectar from flowers like milkweed. They have a wingspan of about 3.5–4in (8.8–10cm) and weigh around 0.02oz (0.5g). Their lifespan is usually around 2–6 weeks, but migrating monarchs can live up to 8 months. Monarchs are known for their incredible long-distance migration every year. They belong to the ***Nymphalidae*** family, and their scientific name is ***Danaus plexippus***.

DID YOU KNOW?

They can fly up to 3,000 miles during their migration to warmer places in Mexico.

SWALLOWTAIL BUTTERFLY

The Swallowtail Butterfly is known for its bright colors, often with black, yellow, blue or red markings on its wings. These butterflies are herbivores. As caterpillars, they feed on plants like parsley and dill, while adults drink nectar from flowers. They have a wingspan of about 3–5in (7.6–12.7cm). Their lifespan is around a few weeks, and they are famous for the tail-like extensions on their wings that resemble a swallow's tail. They belong to the ***Papilionidae*** family, and are a member of the ***Papilio*** genus.

DID YOU KNOW?

There are more than 500 species of Swallowtails found worldwide, except in the Arctic region.

PAINTED LADY BUTTERFLY

The Painted Lady Butterfly is a colorful butterfly with orange wings, black and white spots and brown patterns on the underside. These butterflies are herbivores, feeding on nectar from flowers like thistles and daisies. Painted Ladies have a wingspan of about 2–3in (5–7.6cm). Their lifespan is short, lasting only about 2–4 weeks. They are known for their long migrations across regions. They belong to the ***Nymphalidae*** family, and their scientific name is ***Vanessa cardui***.

DID YOU KNOW?

These butterflies can be found on every continent except Antarctica.

WESTERN PYGMY BLUE BUTTERFLY

The Western Pygmy Blue Butterfly is one of the smallest butterflies in the world. It has a beautiful mix of brown and copper colors on its wings, with tiny blue spots. It's a herbivore, feeding on plants like saltbush and pickleweed. The butterfly is very small, with a wingspan of about 0.5–0.7in (1.2–1.9cm). It has a short lifespan of just a few weeks. This butterfly belongs to the ***Lycaenidae*** family, and its scientific name is ***Brephidium exilis***.

DID YOU KNOW?

Being one of the tiniest, its size is relatively smaller than that of a fingernail.

CABBAGE WHITE BUTTERFLY

The Cabbage White Butterfly is mostly white with small black spots on its wings. These butterflies are herbivores, feeding on nectar from flowers, and their caterpillars munch on cabbage and other leafy plants. They grow to about 1.5–2in (3.8–5cm) in wingspan and are lightweight. Their lifespan is short, that lasts up to 2–3 weeks, and they are often seen fluttering in gardens and fields. They belong to the ***Pieridae*** family, and their scientific name is ***Pieris rapae***.

DID YOU KNOW?

Cabbage Whites can fly up to 30mi (48km) in search of food!

OWL BUTTERFLY

The Owl Butterfly is known for its large wings with eye-like spots that look like an owl's eyes. Their wings are a blend of brown, tan and cream with striking eye spots. Herbivores by nature, Owl Butterflies mainly feed on fruits like bananas. They can grow up to 5–6in (12.7–15.2cm) wide, making them one of the largest butterflies. Their lifespan is short, lasting only around 3–4 weeks. These butterflies belong to the ***Nymphalidae*** family, and to the ***Caligo*** genus.

DID YOU KNOW?

The owl-like eyes on their wings help them defend themselves against predators.

GLASSWING BUTTERFLY

The Glasswing Butterfly is a unique insect with see-through wings. Its wings have clear, glassy sections bordered by brown, orange or white edges. It is a herbivore and feeds on nectar from flowers. The Glasswing Butterfly has a wingspan of about 2–3in (5–7.6cm). After turning into an adult, it can live for about 2–3 weeks in the wild. Its transparent wings help it stay safe from predators by blending it with its environment. This butterfly belongs to the ***Nymphalidae*** family, and its scientific name is ***Greta oto***.

DID YOU KNOW?

Glasswing Butterflies use their wings to regulate body temperature.

LUNA MOTH

The Luna Moth is a large, beautiful moth with pale green wings and long, tail-like extensions. Luna moths are herbivores. As caterpillars, they feed on tree leaves like hickory and walnut. They can grow a wingspan of about 4.5in (11.4cm), making them one of the largest moths in North America. They only live for about a week as adults, during which they don't eat and focus solely on mating. They belong to the family ***Saturniidae***, and their scientific name is ***Actias luna***.

DID YOU KNOW?

Adult Luna Moths lack mouth and digestive system and live on the energy stored as a caterpillar.

ATLAS MOTH

The Atlas Moth is one of the largest moths in the world, with wings that are reddish-brown with striking white, black and orange patterns. As adults, these moths don't eat; they live off the energy stored from their caterpillar stage. Their wingspan can reach up to 12in (30.4cm). Their lifespan is short, only about 1–2 weeks as adults. They belong to the ***Saturniidae*** family, and their scientific name is ***Attacus atlas***.

DID YOU KNOW?

The snake-like markings and patterns on the moth can ward off predators.

LOBSTER MOTH

The Lobster Moth gets its name from the odd shape of its caterpillar, which looks like a lobster with its long legs and tail. As an adult, it has grayish-brown wings with wavy patterns. The caterpillars are herbivores, eating leaves from trees like oak and beech. A Lobster Moth can grow up to 1.5–2in (3.8–5cm) long. It has a lifespan of about 6 weeks as adults. This moth belongs to the ***Notodontidae*** family, and its scientific name is ***Stauropus fagi***.

DID YOU KNOW?

Lobster Moths are nocturnal, which means they are active at night.

DEATH'S-HEAD HAWK MOTH

The Death's-Head Hawk Moth is famous for the skull-like pattern on its back. It has dark brown or black wings with yellow markings and bands on its body. It is a nocturnal moth and has an unusual diet, feeding on honey, fruit and nectar. The moth grows to about 5in (12.7cm) in wingspan. Its lifespan is short, lasting only a few weeks. A Death's-Head Hawk belongs to the ***Sphingidae*** family, and its scientific name is ***Acherontia atropos***.

DID YOU KNOW?

This moth makes a squeak sound when they sense danger.

HUMMINGBIRD MOTH

The Hummingbird Moth is a fascinating insect with colors that resemble a hummingbird, usually a mix of brown, green and white. This moth is a pollinator and drinks nectar from flowers using a long, straw-like mouthpart. It's about the size of a real hummingbird, measuring 1.5–2in (3.8–5cm) long, with a wingspan of up to 2in (5cm). It weighs only around 0.1oz (2.8g). The Hummingbird Moth has a short lifespan of about 3–5 weeks, and it's known for flying during the day, just like hummingbirds! It belongs to the ***Sphingidae*** family.

DID YOU KNOW?

Hummingbird Moths can hover midair, just like hummingbirds!

WOOD ANT

The Wood Ant is usually reddish-brown with a black head and abdomen. These ants are omnivores, meaning they eat both plants and animals. They feed on small insects and love sugary substances like honeydew from aphids. Wood Ants grow to about 0.2–0.4in (0.5–1cm) long. They can live up to 7 years. They belong to the ***Formicidae*** family, and their scientific name is ***Formica rufa***.

BLACK GARDEN ANT

The Black Garden Ant is shiny black in color. These ants are omnivores, meaning they eat a variety of foods, including small insects, nectar and sweet substances like honeydew from aphids. They are small, measuring about 0.1–0.2in (0.25–0.5cm) long. Black Garden Ants can live for more than 15 years, with queens living even longer. They are commonly found in gardens and lawns. They belong to the ***Formicidae*** family, and their scientific name is ***Lasius niger***.

DID YOU KNOW?

These ants communicate using chemical signals called pheromones.

VELVET ANT

The Velvet Ant, despite its name, is actually a type of wasp and not an ant at all! These fascinating insects are usually bright red or orange with a velvety texture on their bodies. Velvet Ants are carnivores, feeding mainly on the larvae of bees and other insects. They typically measure about 0.2–0.8in (0.5–2cm). long and weigh around 0.02oz (0.5g). The queens have a lifespan of over 20 years while the worker ants survive for about 2–3 years. Their sting is very powerful making them a unique but dangerous creature to encounter! They belong to the ***Mutillidae*** family, and their scientific name can vary among species.

ARMY ANT

The Army Ant is mostly reddish-brown or black in color. These ants are carnivores, hunting other insects and small animals as they march in large groups. Their large jaws called mandibles help them slice their prey. Army Ants can be about 0.2–0.6in (0.5–1.5cm) long, and although they are small, they work together, making them a powerful force. Their lifespan is typically a few months, but queens can live longer. Army Ants are famous for their teamwork, even creating living bridges with their bodies to cross gaps during their raids! They are of the ***Formicidae*** family and belong to the genus ***Eciton***.

FIRE ANT

The Fire Ant is a reddish-brown ant known for its painful sting. Fire Ants are omnivores, eating a mix of plants, seeds and other insects. They typically measure about 0.12–0.25in (0.3–0.6cm) long. The worker Fire Ants have a shorter lifespan of a few months only, compared to the queen ant who lives to over 6 years. These ants build large, visible mounds in the ground and are known for their aggressive behavior when their nests are disturbed. They belong to the ***Formicidae*** family, and are of the genus ***Solenopsis***.

DID YOU KNOW?

Fire Ants are great at swimming; they can form rafts to stay afloat!

LEAFCUTTER ANT

The Leafcutter Ant is reddish-brown and is famous for cutting and carrying pieces of leaves. They are herbivores but don't eat the leaves directly. Instead, they use the leaves to grow a special fungus, which they eat. Leafcutter Ants are small, about 0.08–0.7in (0.2–1.9cm) long. The average lifespan of these ants is around 7–9 years and are known for their teamwork and strength. These ants belong to the ***Formicidae*** family.

DID YOU KNOW?
These ants can carry leaves 50 times their weight!

BLACK WIDOW SPIDER

The Black Widow Spider has its skeleton outside the body. The female Black Widow has a shiny black body with a red hourglass shape on its belly while the males are gray or brown having red spots over their body. It is a carnivore, feeding mostly on insects like flies, mosquitoes and beetles, which it catches in its web. A Black Widow is small, about 1.5in (3.8cm) long. Females live up to 3 years, while males live for a few months. Despite its fearsome reputation, it rarely bites humans and prefers to stay hidden in dark, quiet places. This spider belongs to the ***Theridiidae*** family, and is member of the genus ***Latrodectus***.

WOLF SPIDER

The Wolf Spider is typically brown, gray or black with dark stripes or markings, helping it blend into its surroundings. These spiders are carnivores, hunting insects and small bugs. Wolf Spiders are about 1–2in (2.5–5cm) in size They have a lifespan of up to 2 years. Unlike most spiders, they chase their prey on the ground instead of spinning webs to catch food. They belong to the ***Lycosidae*** family, with several species spread worldwide.

DID YOU KNOW?

Female Wolf Spiders carry their baby spiders on their backs until they become independent.

BROWN RECLUSE SPIDER

The Brown Recluse Spider is a small, light yellow to dark brown spider with a distinctive violin-shaped mark on the upper half of its body. These spiders are carnivorous, feeding mainly on insects like ants, flies and beetles. Brown recluses are about 0.2–0.5in (0.5–1.2cm) in size. They can live for more than 3 years. These spiders are shy and prefer hiding in dark places like basements or closets. They belong to the ***Sicariidae*** family, and their scientific name is ***Loxosceles reclusa***.

DID YOU KNOW?

They are not aggressive and attack humans only when threatened.

CRAB SPIDER

The Crab Spider is named after its crab-like shape and movements. They come in various colors, like yellow, white, gray or brown, which help them blend with flowers to catch prey. They are carnivores, eating insects like flies, bees and butterflies. Crab Spiders are small, about 0.2–0.4in (0.5–1cm) long. They typically live for a year and are excellent ambush hunters. These spiders belong to the ***Thomisidae*** family.

DID YOU KNOW?

Crab Spiders use their long front legs to grab insects like crabs do with their claws.

DID YOU KNOW?

Some Ghost Spiders can be quite large, with a leg span of up to 2in (5cm)!

GHOST SPIDER

The Ghost Spider is usually pale white or light yellow, giving it a spooky, ghost-like appearance. These spiders are carnivorous, feeding on small insects at night. Ghost Spiders are small, with a size of around 0.2–0.4in (0.5–1cm). They are very light, weighing less than 0.01oz (0.3g). Their lifespan is typically about a year, and they are known for their fast movements. They belong to the ***Anyphaenidae*** family, and are members of the genus ***Anyphaena***.

ORB-WEAVER

The Orb-Weaver Spider is known for its bright colors, ranging from yellow and orange to brown and black. They are arachnids and spin large, circular webs to catch their food. Orb-Weavers are carnivores, eating insects like flies and beetles. They are usually about 0.2–1in (0.5–2.5cm) long, depending on the species, and weigh about 0.01oz (0.3g). These spiders have a lifespan of around a year, and you can often spot them hanging in gardens or forests, waiting for their next meal! These spiders belong to the ***Araneidae*** family, comprising various species like the Garden Spiders. Their scientific name is ***Araneus diadematus***.

DID YOU KNOW?

Many Orb-Weavers build their webs at night and take them down during the day.

SWALLOWTAIL CATERPILLAR

The Swallowtail Caterpillar, often brightly colored, can be green, yellow or even black, depending on the species. At this larval stage, it primarily feeds on leaves from plants like parsley, dill and fennel. Swallowtail Caterpillars grow to about 3–4in (7.6–10cm) long and weigh only a few ounces. Their lifespan lasts several weeks before they pupate into beautiful butterflies. They belong to the ***Papilionidae*** family, with the scientific name varying by species, such as ***Papilio machaon*** for the Eastern Swallowtail.

DID YOU KNOW?

Some Swallowtail Caterpillars have "horns" on their bodies that can confuse predators.

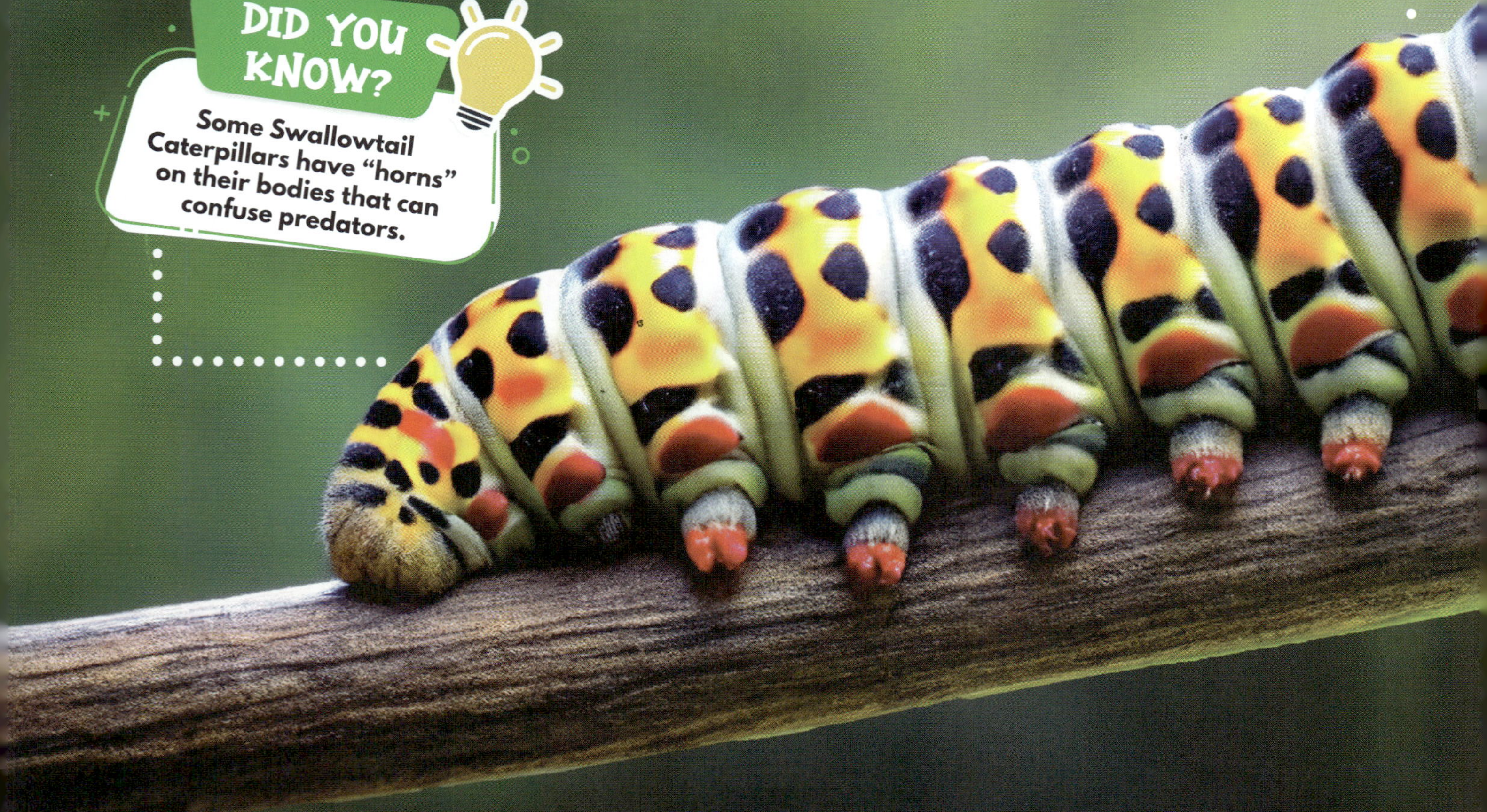

PINE EMPEROR CATERPILLAR

The Pine Emperor Caterpillar is a bright green caterpillar with yellow and black markings. It is a herbivore, feeding mainly on pine needles. As it grows, it can reach about 3–4in (7.6–10cm) long. The caterpillar is relatively light, weighing just a few ounces. Its lifespan as a caterpillar is a few weeks before it forms a cocoon and transforms into a beautiful moth with large wings. It belongs to the ***Saturniidae*** family, and its scientific name is ***Imbrasia cytheris***.

DID YOU KNOW?

They often visually mimic bird droppings to avoid being eaten by predators.

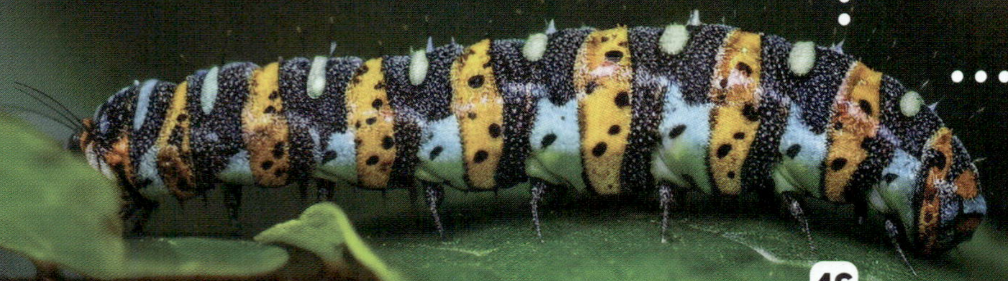

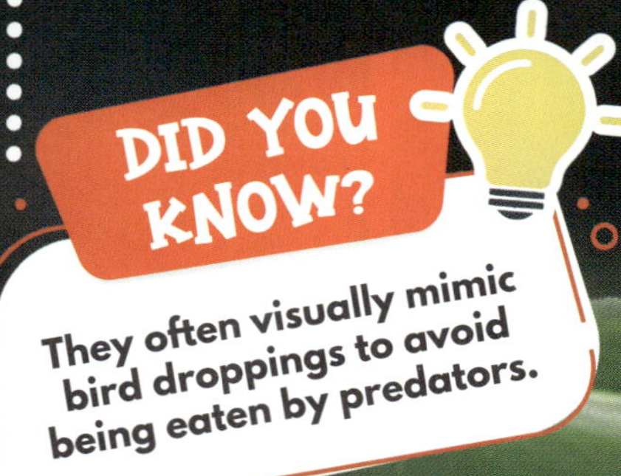

WOOLLY BEAR CATERPILLAR

The Woolly Bear Caterpillar is famous for its fuzzy appearance, with bands of black and orange-brown fur. These caterpillars are the larval stage of the Isabella Tiger Moths. They are herbivores, feeding on a variety grass, clover and leaves. Woolly Bears are about 2in (5cm) long and weigh a few ounces. They can live up to 7 years, especially in cold climates. In fact, Woolly bears are known for their ability to survive freezing temperatures! They belong to the ***Arctiidae*** family, and their scientific name is ***Pyrrharctia isabella***.

DID YOU KNOW?

The band size on Woolly Bears can indicate the harshness of winter.

COCKROACH

The Cockroach is usually brown or black in color. They are the type of insects that eat almost anything, including plants, food scraps and even paper! Cockroaches range in size from 1–2in (2.5–5cm) long. They can live for around a year. These insects are known for surviving in different environments! Cockroaches belong to a number of families depending upon their region of habitat and are of the ***Blattodea*** order.

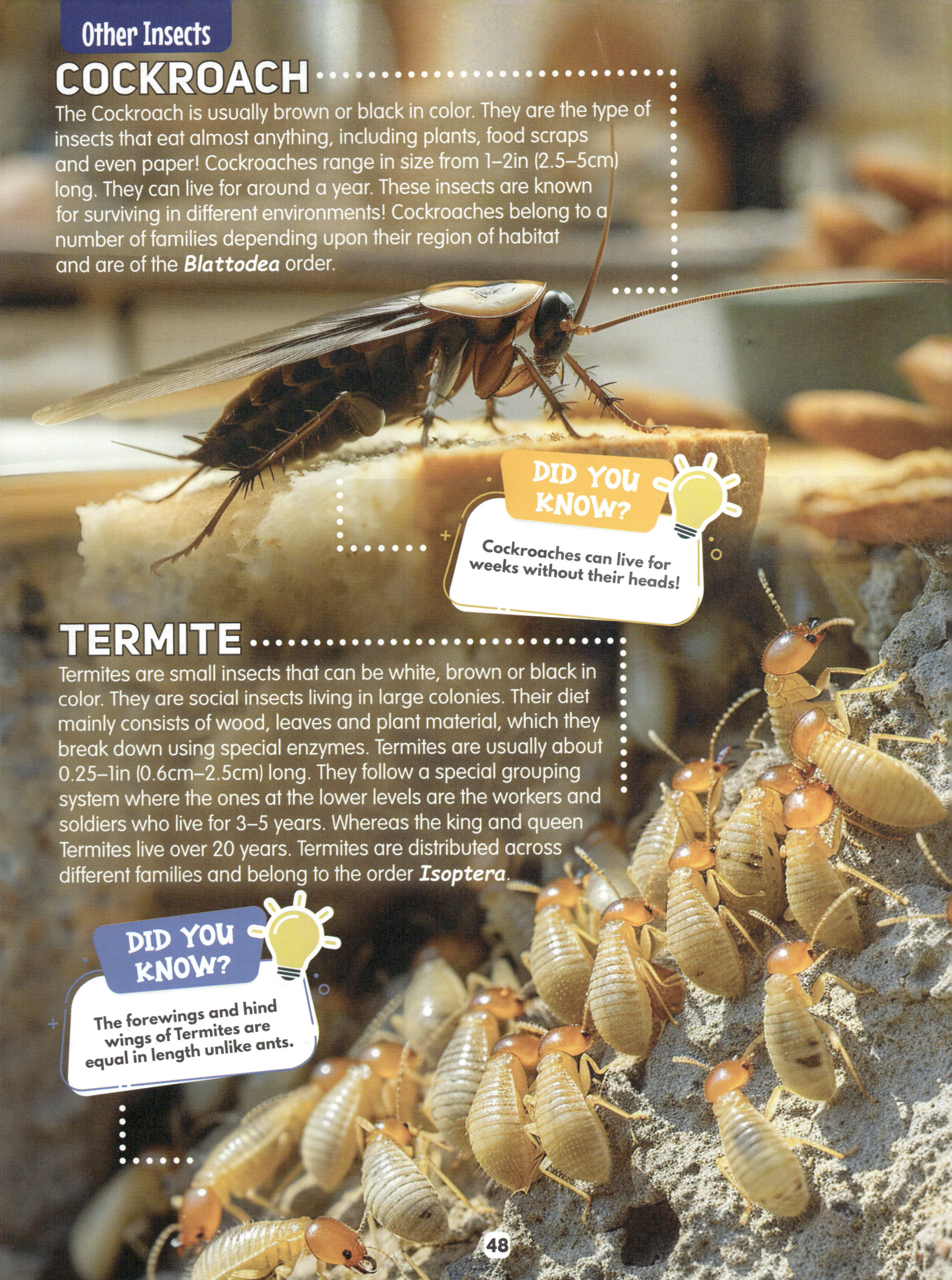

DID YOU KNOW?

Cockroaches can live for weeks without their heads!

TERMITE

Termites are small insects that can be white, brown or black in color. They are social insects living in large colonies. Their diet mainly consists of wood, leaves and plant material, which they break down using special enzymes. Termites are usually about 0.25–1in (0.6cm–2.5cm) long. They follow a special grouping system where the ones at the lower levels are the workers and soldiers who live for 3–5 years. Whereas the king and queen Termites live over 20 years. Termites are distributed across different families and belong to the order ***Isoptera***.

DID YOU KNOW?

The forewings and hind wings of Termites are equal in length unlike ants.